EMBRACE THE TIMELESS WISDOM OF SENECA

TRANSFORM YOUR LIFE BY CONQUERING FEAR AND FINDING PURPOSE

John Sanchez

To my dear daughter Karina,

May the wisdom within these pages inspire you to courageously face your fears, pursue your passions, and lead a life filled with purpose and fulfillment.

With all my love and support,

Dad

"Difficulties strengthen the mind, as labor does the body."

- SENECA

CONTENTS

INTRODUCTION

Embrace Your Fears, Discover Your Purpose

I n today's fast-paced world, it's easy to get caught up in the hustle and bustle of daily life. We often find ourselves feeling overwhelmed, anxious, and fearful of the unknown. The constant pressure to succeed, whether personally or professionally, can lead to a sense of unease and dissatisfaction. But what if we could learn to embrace our fears and use them as a catalyst for growth and self-discovery? This book will explore strategies and insights that can help you transform your fears into purpose and fulfillment.

Why should you care about facing your fears and discovering your purpose? The answer is simple: when you live a life driven by purpose, you are more likely to feel fulfilled, happy, and content. Research has shown that individuals with a strong sense of purpose experience greater life satisfaction, improved mental and physical health, and increased resilience in the face of adversity. By learning to harness the power of fear and channel it towards positive change, you can unlock your full potential and lead a more meaningful, rewarding life.

So, how can you begin to confront your fears and uncover your true purpose? One way is to examine your stories about your fears and limitations. These narratives are often deeply ingrained in our subconscious and can shape our beliefs, attitudes, and behaviors. By challenging these stories and reframing your mindset, you can break free from the constraints of fear and develop a greater sense of self-awareness.

Do you ever wonder why certain fears hold you back while others propel you forward? The following sections will explore the different types of fear and their underlying causes. We will also discuss practical strategies for overcoming fear and building the courage to face life's challenges head-on. By understanding the nature of fear and learning to harness its power, you can unlock your full potential and create lasting, positive change in your life.

What role does purpose play in our lives, and how can we discover our own unique purpose? In the next section, we will discuss the importance of purpose and explore various tools and techniques for uncovering your passions and interests. We will also examine the role of personal values in guiding your actions and decisions, helping you create a life aligned with your true purpose.

How can you use your newfound sense of purpose to drive positive change in your life and the lives of those around you? In the following sections, we will explore the power of purpose-driven action and discuss practical strategies for turning your dreams into reality. We will also examine the role of mindset, motivation, and resilience in overcoming obstacles and achieving your goals.

Are you ready to embark on this journey of self-discovery and transformation? As you read through the pages of this book, I encourage you to approach each chapter with an open mind and a willingness to embrace change. By actively engaging with the exercises and reflections provided, you can begin to cultivate the skills and mindset needed to face your fears, discover your purpose, and lead a fulfilling, purpose-driven life.

What can you expect to gain from this journey? As you work through the chapters, you will learn valuable insights and strategies for overcoming fear, cultivating self-awareness, and discovering your unique purpose. You will also develop the tools and techniques needed to create lasting, positive change in your life and the lives of those around you. So, let's begin this journey together – are you ready to embrace your fears and uncover your true purpose?

PREFACE

Facing Fears, Finding Purpose

As the CEO of several companies and the author of this book, I am passionate about helping individuals and businesses find their purpose. But my journey towards purpose was not always clear or straightforward.

In my mid-thirties, I faced a major turning point in my life when I was unexpectedly fired from a lucrative sales job that paid a quarter of a million dollars per year. This event served as a wake-up call. Over the next 18 months, I took on a few high-paying sales positions, but my heart was no longer in it. Something was missing, and I couldn't ignore the growing sense of discontent.

During this time, the internet emerged as a breeding ground for visionaries and entrepreneurs who were passionately pursuing their dreams. Fortuitously, I had the opportunity to consult with some of these trailblazers in the early days of the Internet, assisting them with business strategies and marketing efforts. Although I didn't realize it at the time, I discovered that I had a knack for helping these entrepreneurs find and fulfill their potential.

As my consultancy evolved into a full-fledged digital marketing agency, I recognized my talent for assisting businesses and identifying potential in individuals, coaching them, and placing them in positions where they could thrive and succeed.

In my late thirties, I found myself at a crossroads, unsure of which direction to take. I decided to take a leap of faith and align my work with my newfound passion for helping others find and fulfill their potential. The experience of being fired and the subsequent journey into entrepreneurship opened my eyes to the diverse range of passions and talents that exist beyond traditional career paths.

This entrepreneurial journey taught me that my purpose extended beyond running a successful company. Instead, I found immense satisfaction and meaning in empowering and inspiring others to pursue their dreams and overcome their fears.

Through my work with Zunch-related companies and my writing and speaking engagements, I have had the privilege of connecting with people from all walks of life on their journey toward purpose. I have seen firsthand the transformative power of aligning one's actions with their purpose, and I am committed to helping as many people as possible achieve that alignment.

In this book, I have distilled my years of experience and knowledge into a step-by-step guide to help you discover and live your purpose. I hope my journey and the lessons I have learned will inspire and guide you on your journey toward fulfillment and purpose.

Thank you for choosing "Embrace the Timeless Wisdom of Seneca: Transform Your Life by Conquering Fear and Finding Purpose." I am honored to be a part of your journey.

John Sanchez
April 2023

CHAPTER 1.
UNDERSTANDING
SENECA'S WISDOM

Who was Lucius Annaeus Seneca?

The Life Of A Stoic Philosopher

Lucius Annaeus Seneca, often referred to simply as Seneca, was a Roman philosopher, statesman, and playwright. Born in Corduba, Spain, in 4 BC, Seneca received his education in Rome, where he later rose to prominence as a skilled orator, moral philosopher, and political advisor. Seneca was a prominent figure in the Roman Empire, serving as a tutor and advisor to Emperor Nero. Although he ultimately faced a tragic end, forced to commit suicide by the very emperor he mentored, Seneca's wisdom and teachings have transcended time.

Why should you care about Seneca's life? By understanding the historical context in which Seneca lived and worked, you can better appreciate his profound insights, which remain relevant to our lives today. Furthermore, his experiences shaped his philosophical views, providing context for his thoughts on fear, imagination, and personal fulfillment.

Seneca's Writings And Contributions

Seneca was a prolific writer, and his works spanned diverse genres, including tragedy, satire, and essays. Among his most famous works are his philosophical essays, such as "On the Shortness of Life," "On the Happy Life," and "Letters from a Stoic." These writings have had a lasting impact on Western philosophy and continue to inspire readers today.

What makes Seneca's writings so valuable? His works offer practical advice on how to live a virtuous life, and they address a wide range of topics, including happiness, friendship, anger, and fear. By studying his works, you can gain a deeper understanding of human nature and practical guidance on overcoming personal obstacles and living a more fulfilling life.

"We are more often frightened than hurt, and suffer more in imagination than in reality."

"We are more often frightened than hurt, and suffer more in imagination than in reality."

The Power Of Fear And Imagination

Seneca's quote speaks to the human tendency to magnify our fears in our minds, often causing us to suffer more from our thoughts than from the actual events we face. This insight is critical because it reveals that much of our suffering is self-inflicted, resulting from our imaginations running wild.

Why should this matter to you? By recognizing the role that fears and imagination play in your life, you can begin to take control of your thoughts and emotions. Instead of allowing your fears to dictate your actions, you can learn to confront them head-on and make decisions based on rational analysis rather than irrational anxieties.

Facing Fear: A Path To Personal Growth

Seneca's wisdom suggests overcoming our fears by acknowledging their power over us and learning to manage our imaginations. This process is crucial to personal growth, as it allows us to confront the obstacles that stand in our way and develop resilience in the face of adversity.

Why is facing fear so essential? When you confront your fears, you open yourself up to new experiences and opportunities for growth. By challenging your limits and pushing past your comfort zone, you can unlock your true potential and become the best version of yourself.

But how can you begin to face your fears and overcome the limitations imposed by your imagination? This question prompts us to explore the philosophical foundation that underpins Seneca's wisdom: Stoicism.

Stoicism and its Impact on
Modern Thinking

The Core Principles Of Stoicism

Stoicism is an ancient Greek philosophy founded by Zeno of Citium in the early 3rd century BC. It teaches that the key to a happy and fulfilling life is cultivating virtue and developing self-control over one's thoughts, emotions, and actions. Stoicism emphasizes the importance of rational thinking, emotional resilience, and personal responsibility. By practicing these principles, Stoics believe that individuals can achieve inner peace and contentment, regardless of their external circumstances.

Why should you care about Stoicism? This philosophical approach provides a practical framework for self-improvement that we can apply to modern life. By embracing Stoic principles, you can learn to manage your fears, control your imagination, and develop the mental fortitude needed to overcome life's challenges.

Stoicism In Modern Life

Stoicism has experienced a resurgence in recent years thanks to its practical and accessible teachings. Successful entrepreneurs, athletes, and leaders across various fields have adopted its principles to enhance their mental resilience, focus, and overall well-being.

Why is Stoicism so relevant today? Many people struggle with stress, anxiety, and feeling overwhelmed in our fast-paced, increasingly connected world. Stoicism offers a time-tested approach to managing these challenges, helping individuals cultivate a calm, rational mindset and maintain balance.

But how can Stoicism help you overcome fear and unlock your full potential? This question brings us to the crucial relationship between Stoicism and fear and the role confronting fear plays in living a fulfilling life.

The Importance of Overcoming Fear

Stoicism And Fear: A Path To Mastery

Stoicism teaches that fear is a product of irrational thinking and misplaced value judgments. By developing self-awareness and rational analysis, you can identify the source of your fears, question their validity, and ultimately, diminish their power over your life. This process is essential for personal growth, as it enables you to confront the obstacles that hinder your progress and develop the resilience needed to persevere through adversity.

Why should you care about mastering your fears? By confronting and overcoming your fears, you unlock new opportunities for growth and self-discovery. This process can lead to increased confidence, improved decision-making, and greater fulfillment in your personal and professional life.

Overcoming Fear: The Key To Unlocking Your Potential

As Seneca's quote suggests, our fears often cause us more suffering than the events we face. By overcoming your fears, you can free yourself from the self-imposed limitations that hold you back and begin to unlock your full potential. This process is essential for personal growth and finding and pursuing your life's purpose.

Why is overcoming fear vital for finding your purpose? Fear can prevent you from exploring new opportunities, taking risks, and pursuing your passions. By learning to manage and confront your fears, you can break free from these constraints and embark on a journey of self-discovery that will ultimately lead you to a more fulfilling life.

But how can you apply Seneca's wisdom and Stoicism to your life to conquer your fears and find your purpose? This question sets the stage for the following chapters, where we will explore practical strategies and techniques for facing your fears, discovering your life's purpose, and embracing a fulfilling existence.

CHAPTER 2. THE NATURE OF FEAR AND IMAGINATION

Defining Fear: Types and Causes

Understanding The Essence Of Fear

F ear is a fundamental human emotion that responds to perceived threats or dangers. It is a natural survival mechanism that has evolved to help us avoid harm and navigate uncertain situations. To better manage and overcome fear, it is essential to understand its types and causes.

Why should you care about understanding fear? By gaining insight into the nature of fear, you can identify the specific triggers that affect you and develop targeted strategies for managing and confronting these fears.

Types Of Fear

There are several types of fear, including:

Realistic fears: These fears are rooted in actual threats or dangers, such as fear of physical harm, accidents, or natural disasters. They serve a practical purpose, helping us stay alert and respond effectively to potential threats.

Irrational fears: Imaginations, past experiences, or cultural influences fuel these fears, which do not stem from actual or immediate threats. Examples include fear of public speaking, fear of failure, or fear of rejection.

Existential fears: These fears are related to our mortality, the meaning of life, and the unknown. They can include fear of death, fear of insignificance, or fear of the uncertain future.

Why is it important to recognize the types of fear? By categorizing your fears, you can better understand their origins and develop targeted strategies for addressing them, ultimately enhancing your ability to cope with and overcome fear.

Causes Of Fear

Fear can arise from various sources, including:

Genetics: Some individuals may have a genetic predisposition to heightened anxiety and fear responses.

Past experiences: Traumatic events or negative experiences can instill fear and condition us to react with fear in similar situations.

Environment and culture: Our upbringing, social environment, and cultural norms can influence the development of specific fears.

Cognitive processes: Our thought patterns, beliefs, and expectations can contribute to the manifestation of fear.

Why should you care about the causes of fear? By understanding the underlying factors contributing to fear, you can develop a deeper awareness of your emotions and take proactive steps to manage and confront your fears.

The Role of Imagination in Creating Fear

Imagination: A Double-Edged Sword

Imagination is a powerful human faculty that allows us to envision possibilities, create new ideas, and escape the confines of our current reality. However, this creative force can also be a source of fear when it conjures up worst-case scenarios or imagined threats.

Why should you care about the role of imagination in fear? By recognizing the power of your imagination to create fear, you can take control of your thoughts and develop strategies to counteract the adverse effects of your imagination.

The Mind's Eye: Fueling Fear

Our imagination can generate fear by amplifying our perceived threats, magnifying their potential consequences, or creating fictional scenarios. This process can cause us to experience fear and anxiety even when there is no real danger.

Why is understanding the mind's role in fear important? By acknowledging your imagination's role in generating fear, you can learn to separate imagined threats from real ones and challenge the validity of your fears.

But what are the consequences of letting fear dictate our lives?

This question leads us to explore the impact of fear on our well-being, relationships, and overall life satisfaction.

The Consequences of Letting Fear Dictate Our Lives

Fear's Grip On Our Lives

Allowing fear to control our thoughts and actions can have far-reaching consequences on various aspects of our lives. Fear can prevent us from pursuing our passions, taking risks, and embracing new experiences. It can also hinder our personal growth, limit our potential, and diminish our overall well-being.

Why should you care about the consequences of fear? By understanding the negative impact of fear on your life, you can appreciate the importance of confronting and overcoming your fears to achieve a more fulfilling existence.

Lost Opportunities And Regrets

One of the most significant consequences of letting fear dictate our lives is the loss of opportunities for growth, learning, and success. Fear can cause us to avoid challenges, resist change, and settle for mediocrity. Over time, this can lead to feelings of regret as we reflect on missed opportunities and unfulfilled potential.

Why is understanding lost opportunities important? By recognizing the potential cost of letting fear control your life, you can find the motivation to face your fears and seize the opportunities that come your way.

Impaired Relationships And Social Isolation

Fear can also negatively impact our relationships and social lives. When consumed by fear, we may avoid social situations, shy away from forming new connections, or struggle to maintain existing relationships. Experiencing such fears can lead to social isolation, loneliness, and a reduced support network.

Why should you care about the impact of fear on relationships? Healthy relationships and social connections are essential components of a fulfilling life. Confronting and managing your fears can strengthen your relationships and enhance your social well-being.

But how can we better understand the relationship between fear and imagination? This question leads us to explore psychological theories on fear and imagination.

Psychological Theories on Fear and Imagination

Cognitive-Behavioral Theory

Cognitive-behavioral theory posits that our thoughts, emotions, and behaviors are interconnected. According to this theory, fear arises from distorted or irrational thought patterns, which our imagination can fuel. These thoughts then influence our emotions and behaviors, perpetuating the cycle of fear.

Why should you care about cognitive-behavioral theory? This theory provides a framework for understanding the role of imagination in creating fear and offers practical strategies for challenging and changing negative thought patterns to alleviate fear and anxiety.

Classical Conditioning

Classical conditioning is a psychological theory explaining how associations can teach fear. In this process, a neutral stimulus becomes associated with a fearful event or outcome, leading to a conditioned fear response. This theory helps to explain how our past experiences can influence our present fears and anxieties.

Why is understanding classical conditioning important? By recognizing the role of conditioning in the development of fear, you can identify and challenge the associations that contribute to your fears, ultimately helping to reduce their intensity and impact on your life.

The Role Of The Amygdala

The amygdala, a small almond-shaped structure in the brain, plays a critical role in processing fear and emotional memories. When the amygdala perceives a threat, it triggers a fear response, preparing the body for action. However, the amygdala can also respond to imagined threats, causing us to experience fear even without real danger.

Why should you care about the amygdala's role in fear? Understanding the neurological basis of fear can help you appreciate the complex interplay between your brain, imagination, and emotions and empower you to develop strategies for managing and overcoming fear.

How can you apply these psychological theories to confront your fears and harness the power of your imagination for personal growth and fulfillment? This question sets the stage for the following chapters, where we will explore practical techniques and strategies for facing your fears, managing your imagination, and, ultimately, discovering and pursuing your life's purpose.

CHAPTER 3. FINDING YOUR PURPOSE

*The Concept of Purpose
and Meaning in Life*

The Quest For Purpose

The search for purpose and meaning is a fundamental aspect of human existence. Our purpose represents the driving force that motivates us, provides direction, and imbues our lives with a sense of meaning and fulfillment. By understanding the concept of purpose, you can explore your path and discover what truly matters to you.

Why should you care about the concept of purpose? Recognizing the importance of purpose can inspire you to embark on a journey of self-discovery, leading you to uncover your unique passions, values, and aspirations, ultimately enhancing your overall life satisfaction.

Meaning In Life

Meaning in life refers to the sense of coherence, significance, and purpose individuals derive from their experiences, relationships, and activities. Finding meaning is essential for psychological well-being and can contribute to greater happiness, resilience, and overall life satisfaction.

Why is understanding meaning in life important? By appreciating the significance of meaning, you can prioritize the activities, relationships, and pursuits that genuinely enrich your life, fostering a more profound sense of fulfillment and contentment.

But what are the common obstacles that prevent us from discovering our purpose? This question leads us to explore the challenges hindering our journey toward self-discovery and purpose.

Common Obstacles in Discovering One's Purpose

Fear And Doubt

As discussed in the previous chapters, fear can be a significant barrier to discovering and pursuing our purpose. Fear of failure, rejection, or change can prevent us from exploring new opportunities, taking risks, and embracing our passions. Doubt can also undermine our confidence in our abilities, making recognizing and pursuing our purpose difficult.

Why should you care about overcoming fear and doubt? By confronting and managing these emotions, you can break free from their constraints and gain the courage and confidence to uncover and pursue your life's purpose.

Lack Of Self-Awareness

Another common obstacle in discovering one's purpose is a lack of self-awareness. Many people struggle to identify their core values, passions, and strengths, making it challenging to recognize their purpose and align their actions accordingly.

Why is self-awareness crucial in discovering your purpose? Developing self-awareness enables you to understand your unique attributes, which can guide you in identifying and pursuing your life's purpose.

External Pressures And Expectations

External pressures and expectations from family, friends, and society can also hinder our ability to discover and pursue our purpose. We may feel compelled to conform to social norms, pursue careers that do not align with our passions or prioritize the expectations of others over our desires.

Why should you care about addressing external pressures and expectations? Recognizing and challenging these influences allows you to develop the autonomy and self-assurance needed to pursue your unique path and purpose.

But how can we overcome these obstacles and uncover our life's purpose? This question leads us to explore strategies for discovering your purpose and aligning it with your values and passions.

Strategies for Uncovering Your Life's Purpose

Self-Reflection And Introspection

Self-reflection and introspection are essential tools for discovering your purpose. By exploring your values, passions, strengths, and life experiences, you can gain valuable insights into the driving forces that define your unique purpose.

Why should you care about self-reflection and introspection? These processes enable you to develop a deeper understanding of yourself, which can guide you in identifying and pursuing your life's purpose.

Experimentation And Exploration

Experimenting with new activities, interests, and experiences can help uncover your passions and purpose. By stepping outside your comfort zone and embracing curiosity, you can discover new aspects of yourself and the world around you, which can illuminate your path toward purpose.

Why should you care about experimentation and exploration? Engaging in these pursuits allows you to broaden your horizons, uncover hidden talents, and identify the passions that genuinely resonate with you, ultimately guiding you toward your life's purpose.

Seeking Feedback And Mentorship

Seeking feedback and mentorship from others can also be invaluable in discovering your purpose. You can gain fresh perspectives and insights into your strengths, passions, and potential paths by engaging in open and honest conversations with trusted friends, family members, or mentors.

Why should you care about seeking feedback and mentorship? The guidance and support of others can give you the encouragement, motivation, and knowledge needed to identify and pursue your life's purpose.

Setting And Achieving Goals

Setting and achieving goals can help you clarify your purpose and make tangible progress toward realizing your aspirations. Establishing specific, measurable, achievable, relevant, and time-bound (SMART) goals allows you to focus your efforts, monitor your progress, and build momentum toward your purpose.

Why is goal-setting important in discovering your purpose? Goals provide a roadmap for your journey toward purpose, enabling you to take meaningful steps, measure your progress, and, ultimately, achieve a more fulfilling life.

Now that you have uncovered your purpose, how can you align it with your values and passions? This question leads us to examine the process of harmonizing your purpose with your core beliefs and interests.

*Aligning Your Purpose with
Your Values and Passions*

Identifying Your Core Values

Your core values are the fundamental beliefs and principles that guide your thoughts, decisions, and actions. By identifying your core values, you can ensure that your purpose aligns with your deeply held beliefs, resulting in a more authentic and fulfilling life.

Why should you care about identifying your core values? Aligning your purpose with your values ensures that your pursuits genuinely resonate with your beliefs, fostering a more profound sense of fulfillment, satisfaction, and meaning in your life.

Connecting Your Passions To Your Purpose

Your passions are the activities, interests, and pursuits that genuinely excite and inspire you. Connecting your passions to your purpose can infuse your life with enthusiasm, motivation, and joy, making it easier to stay committed to your path and achieve your goals.

Why should you care about connecting your passions to your purpose? Engaging in activities that align with your passions and purpose ensures that your life is filled with energy, excitement, and fulfillment, enhancing your overall well-being and life satisfaction.

Taking Action And Making A Difference

Once you have aligned your purpose with your values and passions, it is essential to take action and make a tangible difference in your life and the lives of others. Pursuing your purpose with dedication and commitment can create positive change, inspire others, and experience a profound sense of meaning and fulfillment.

Why should you care about taking action and making a difference? Actively pursuing your purpose allows you to create a meaningful impact, contributing to the well-being of others and fostering a greater sense of purpose and meaning in your life.

Discovering and aligning your purpose with your values and passions is a transformative journey that can lead to a more fulfilling, authentic, and meaningful life. By understanding the concept of purpose, overcoming common obstacles, employing strategies to uncover your purpose, and harmonizing it with your values and passions, you can embark on a path that truly resonates with your unique identity.

But how can you maintain your newfound sense of purpose and continue to grow and evolve throughout your life? This question sets the stage for the following chapters, where we will explore the importance of lifelong learning, personal growth, and resilience in sustaining a purpose-driven life.

CHAPTER 4.
OVERCOMING FEAR AND EMBRACING REALITY

Techniques for Managing and Conquering Fear

Cognitive Reframing

C ognitive reframing is a powerful technique for managing and conquering fear. It involves changing how you perceive and interpret situations that evoke fear and replacing negative thoughts with more positive and empowering ones. Adopting a new perspective can diminish the intensity of your fear and enhance your ability to cope with challenging situations.

Why should you care about cognitive reframing? This technique can help you transform your mindset, allowing you to face your fears with greater confidence and courage, ultimately enhancing your overall well-being and ability to pursue your purpose.

Exposure Therapy

Exposure therapy is a well-established method for overcoming fear, particularly in the context of phobias and anxiety disorders. It involves gradually and systematically confronting the feared situation or object, allowing you to become desensitized and reduce your anxiety over time.

Why should you care about exposure therapy? By facing your fears head-on and gradually acclimating to them, you can build confidence, resilience, and the ability to manage them effectively, paving the way for personal growth and pursuing your purpose.

Relaxation Techniques

Relaxation techniques, such as deep breathing, progressive muscle relaxation, and visualization, can help you manage fear by reducing the physiological symptoms of anxiety and stress. Regularly practicing these techniques can cultivate a greater sense of calm and control in the face of fear.

Why should you care about relaxation techniques? Mastering these techniques can help you remain composed and centered in the face of fear, enhancing your ability to cope with challenges and confidently pursue your purpose.

But how can mindfulness and meditation contribute to facing fear? This question leads us to explore the benefits of these practices in overcoming fear and embracing reality.

The Benefits of Mindfulness and Meditation in Facing Fear

Mindfulness

Mindfulness is the practice of maintaining a non-judgmental awareness of your thoughts, emotions, and bodily sensations in the present moment. By cultivating mindfulness, you can develop greater emotional intelligence, self-awareness, and the ability to respond to fear and anxiety with composure and clarity.

Why should you care about mindfulness? Mindfulness can help you recognize and manage your fears, enabling you to remain grounded and present, even in challenging situations. This heightened awareness can empower you to face your fears and embrace reality with courage and resilience.

Meditation

Meditation is a practice that involves training your mind to develop focus, awareness, and tranquility. Research has shown that regular meditation reduces stress, anxiety, and fear while enhancing emotional regulation, cognitive function, and overall well-being.

Why should you care about meditation? Incorporating meditation into your daily routine can help you cultivate inner peace and mental clarity, allowing you to face your fears with greater equanimity and courage. This practice can also support personal growth and purpose-driven life by fostering emotional resilience and self-awareness.

Resilience plays a crucial role in overcoming fear and embracing reality. But how can we build resilience through adversity? This question leads us to explore the process of developing mental fortitude in the face of challenges.

Building Resilience Through Adversity

The Role Of Adversity

Adversity can be a powerful catalyst for personal growth and resilience. By facing challenges and navigating difficult situations, you can develop mental fortitude, adaptability, and problem-solving skills to overcome fear and embrace reality.

Why should you care about the role of adversity in building resilience? Embracing adversity as an opportunity for growth can help you develop the mental and emotional strength needed to face your fears, overcome obstacles, and pursue your purpose with determination and courage.

Learning From Failure

Failure is an inevitable part of life and can serve as a valuable learning experience. By reflecting on your failures, identifying areas for improvement, and applying the lessons learned, you can develop resilience and cultivate a growth mindset that embraces challenges and change.

Why should you care about learning from failure? Recognizing the value of failure can help you develop the courage and resilience to face your fears and overcome setbacks on your journey toward personal growth and purpose.

Developing A Support Network

Building a strong support network of friends, family, and mentors can significantly contribute to your resilience in the face of adversity. By surrounding yourself with individuals who believe in your abilities and encourage your growth, you can foster a sense of belonging and confidence that helps you overcome fear and embrace reality.

Why should you care about developing a support network? A strong support network can give you the encouragement, guidance, and resources needed to face your fears and navigate adversity, empowering you to pursue your purpose confidently and continuously.

Embracing vulnerability and self-acceptance is another essential aspect of overcoming fear and embracing reality. But how can we cultivate these qualities? This question leads us to explore the importance of vulnerability and self-acceptance in our personal growth and purpose-driven lives.

Embracing Vulnerability
and Self-Acceptance

The Power Of Vulnerability

Embracing vulnerability involves letting yourself be seen and accepting your imperfections, weaknesses, and emotions without shame or judgment. By cultivating vulnerability, you can develop deeper connections with others, foster self-compassion, and challenge your fears with authenticity and courage.

Why should you care about vulnerability? Embracing vulnerability allows you to confront your fears and challenges honestly and openly, fostering personal growth, self-awareness, and navigating adversity with grace and resilience.

Self-Acceptance

Self-acceptance is the practice of embracing and loving yourself unconditionally, including your strengths, weaknesses, and imperfections. By cultivating self-acceptance, you can develop a strong sense of self-worth, confidence, and emotional resilience, enabling you to face your fears and embrace reality with courage and authenticity.

Why should you care about self-acceptance? Self-acceptance empowers you to face your fears and challenges with self-assurance, fostering personal growth and enhancing your ability to pursue your purpose with determination and perseverance.

Overcoming fear and embracing reality is essential to personal growth and living a purpose-driven life. By mastering techniques for managing fear, cultivating mindfulness and meditation, building resilience through adversity, and embracing vulnerability and self-acceptance, you can develop the courage, resilience, and self-awareness needed to face your fears and navigate the challenges of life with grace and determination.

As we continue our journey toward personal growth and purpose, how can we maintain our newfound sense of courage and resilience? This question sets the stage for the following chapters, where we will explore strategies for sustaining personal growth, fostering lifelong learning, and maintaining a purpose-driven life.

CHAPTER 5. APPLYING SENECA'S WISDOM TO DAILY LIFE

Cultivating a Stoic Mindset

Understanding Stoic Philosophy

To apply Seneca's wisdom to daily life, we must first understand the core principles of Stoic philosophy. Stoicism teaches that we can achieve inner peace and happiness by focusing on what we can control – our thoughts, beliefs, and actions – and accepting what we cannot control, such as external circumstances and the actions of others.

Why should you care about understanding Stoic philosophy? Embracing a Stoic mindset can help you cultivate resilience, inner strength, and emotional intelligence, empowering you to face life's challenges with grace and equanimity.

Practicing Negative Visualization

Negative visualization is a Stoic technique that involves

imagining worst-case scenarios and considering how you would respond to them. This practice can help you develop gratitude for your current circumstances, build emotional resilience, and enhance your ability to cope with adversity.

Why should you care about practicing negative visualization? By contemplating potential challenges and setbacks, you can develop a greater appreciation for your current situation and the mental fortitude needed to face life's uncertainties with courage and resilience.

Focusing On What You Can Control

A fundamental tenet of Stoicism is the distinction between what is within our control and what is not. By focusing your energy on what you can control – your thoughts, beliefs, and actions – and accepting what you cannot, you can develop a greater sense of inner peace and resilience in the face of adversity.

Why should you care about focusing on what you can control? Adopting this Stoic principle can help you manage stress, anxiety, and fear more effectively, enabling you to live a more fulfilling and purpose-driven life.

Cultivating a Stoic mindset is just the beginning; we must also incorporate gratitude and contentment into our lives. But how can we do this? This question leads us to explore the role of gratitude and contentment in applying Seneca's wisdom to daily life.

Incorporating Gratitude and Contentment into Your Life

Practicing Gratitude

Gratitude is the practice of recognizing and appreciating the positive aspects of your life, both large and small. By cultivating gratitude, you can develop a more positive outlook, enhance your overall well-being, and foster a greater sense of contentment in your daily life.

Why should you care about practicing gratitude? Research demonstrates that gratitude links to increased happiness reduced stress, and improved mental and physical health. By incorporating gratitude into your daily routine, you can enhance your ability to face life's challenges with grace and resilience.

Cultivating Contentment

Contentment involves finding satisfaction and peace in your present circumstances, without constantly striving for more or dwelling on what you lack. By cultivating contentment, you can develop a greater appreciation for the simple joys in life and foster a more profound sense of inner peace and happiness.

Why should you care about cultivating contentment? Embracing contentment can help you live a more balanced and fulfilling life, reducing the impact of fear, anxiety, and stress on your overall well-being.

Applying Seneca's Wisdom To Material Possessions

Seneca advised against relying on material possessions for happiness and fulfillment. By focusing on the intrinsic value of experiences, relationships, and personal growth, you can cultivate a sense of contentment and gratitude that transcends material wealth.

Why should you care about applying Seneca's wisdom to

material possessions? Recognizing material wealth's fleeting and impermanent nature can help you prioritize what truly matters in life, leading to greater happiness, fulfillment, and purpose.

To effectively apply Seneca's wisdom to daily life, we must also practice self-reflection and self-awareness. But how can we develop these crucial skills?

Practicing Self-Reflection and Self-Awareness

Journaling As A Tool For Self-Reflection

Journaling is a powerful tool for self-reflection that can help you gain insight into your thoughts, emotions, and behaviors. By regularly writing about your experiences, goals, and challenges, you can develop a deeper understanding of yourself and foster personal growth.

Why should you care about journaling as a tool for self-reflection? Journaling can help you identify patterns and habits, clarify your values and beliefs, and track your progress toward personal and professional goals, empowering you to live a more purpose-driven life.

Mindfulness Meditation And Self-Awareness

Mindfulness meditation is a practice that involves focusing your attention on the present moment without judgment. By cultivating mindfulness, you can develop greater self-awareness, emotional intelligence, and resilience in the face of adversity.

Why should you care about mindfulness meditation and self-awareness? Research has shown that mindfulness meditation can reduce stress, improve mental clarity, and enhance overall well-being, making it a valuable tool for fostering self-awareness and personal growth.

Engaging In Self-Reflection Exercises

In addition to journaling and mindfulness meditation, engaging in self-reflection exercises can help you develop self-awareness and foster personal growth. These exercises include asking yourself thought-provoking questions, seeking feedback from others, or participating in personal development workshops or seminars.

Why should you care about engaging in self-reflection exercises? Regularly engaging in self-reflection can help you identify areas for growth, clarify your values and beliefs, and align your actions with your purpose, empowering you to live a more fulfilling and intentional life.

Incorporating Seneca's wisdom into daily life also requires setting realistic goals and embracing personal growth. But how can we achieve this? This question leads us to explore strategies for goal-setting and personal development.

Setting Realistic Goals and
Embracing Personal Growth

Creating Smart Goals

Setting realistic and achievable goals is essential to applying Seneca's wisdom to daily life. One effective approach to goal-setting is the SMART framework, which involves creating goals that are Specific, Measurable, Achievable, Relevant, and Time-bound.

Why should you care about creating SMART goals? Setting clear, realistic, and well-defined goals can increase your likelihood of success, track your progress, and maintain motivation as you work toward personal and professional growth.

Embracing A Growth Mindset

A growth mindset embodies the belief that one can develop intelligence, talent, and abilities through hard work, dedication, and perseverance. By embracing a growth mindset, you can cultivate resilience, adaptability, and a lifelong love of learning, empowering you to face challenges and setbacks with courage and determination.

Why should you care about embracing a growth mindset? Research has shown that individuals with a growth mindset are more likely to embrace challenges, persist in the face of adversity, and achieve higher levels of success than those with a fixed mindset.

Continuous Learning And Self-Improvement

To fully embrace personal growth and apply Seneca's wisdom to daily life, it's essential to prioritize continuous learning and self-improvement. Personal growth might involve reading books, attending workshops or seminars, seeking mentorship, or participating in online courses to expand your knowledge and skills.

Why should you care about continuous learning and self-improvement? Lifelong learning and self-improvement can enhance your ability to adapt to change, develop new skills, and foster a greater sense of purpose and fulfillment in your daily life.

Applying Seneca's wisdom to daily life involves cultivating a Stoic mindset, incorporating gratitude and contentment, practicing self-reflection and self-awareness, and setting realistic goals while embracing personal growth. Integrating these principles and practices into your daily routine allows you to develop the resilience, inner strength, and emotional intelligence needed to overcome fear, face life's challenges with grace and live a more purpose-driven and fulfilling life.

As you embark on this journey of personal growth and self-discovery, remember that applying Seneca's wisdom is a lifelong process that requires patience, commitment, and dedication. Embrace the challenges and setbacks you encounter along the way as opportunities for growth, and celebrate your successes, both large and small.

By consistently working to incorporate Seneca's wisdom into your daily life, you can develop a greater sense of inner peace, contentment, and fulfillment, ultimately empowering you to live a life that is true to your values, passions, and purpose.

As you continue applying Seneca's wisdom to your daily life, you may wonder how to maintain your progress and grow. What strategies and habits can you adopt to ensure that the wisdom of Seneca becomes an integral part of your life journey? Keep asking yourself these questions, and stay committed to your self-discovery and personal growth path.

CHAPTER 6. SUCCESS STORIES AND REAL-LIFE APPLICATIONS

Personal Anecdotes of Conquering Fear and Finding Purpose

Overcoming Social Anxiety

Imagine a young woman named Sarah who suffered from debilitating social anxiety. Simple tasks like making phone calls or attending social events would leave her paralyzed with fear. One day, Sarah stumbled upon Seneca's quote and realized her fear was holding her back from living a fulfilling life.

Why should you care about Sarah's story? It demonstrates the power of understanding and applying Seneca's wisdom in real-life situations. By embracing the principles of Stoicism, Sarah began to challenge her fears and step outside her comfort zone. Over time, she developed the confidence to pursue her passion for helping others, leading her to a fulfilling career as a therapist.

Finding Purpose After A Career Crisis

Next, consider Mark, a successful executive who, after years of climbing the corporate ladder, found himself questioning the purpose of his work. He felt unfulfilled and disconnected from his true passions. Inspired by Seneca's wisdom, Mark faced his fears and made a drastic career change.

Why should you care about Mark's story? By confronting his fears and embracing the uncertainty of change, Mark discovered his true calling as an environmental activist. He used his skills and experience to create positive change in the world. It illustrates the importance of aligning one's actions with their purpose to achieve a meaningful and fulfilling life.

How can we learn from historical figures who embraced Seneca's wisdom? This question leads us to explore the lessons we can draw from their lives.

Lessons From Historical Figures Who Embraced Seneca's Wisdom

Eleanor Roosevelt: Overcoming Fear and Embracing Change

Eleanor Roosevelt, former First Lady of the United States and human rights advocate, famously said, "You gain strength, courage, and confidence by every experience in which you really stop to look fear in the face." Throughout her life, she faced numerous challenges, including personal tragedies and political upheaval, yet she consistently demonstrated the courage and resilience that Seneca's wisdom encourages.

Why should you care about Eleanor Roosevelt's story? Her life provides a powerful example of the transformative impact of facing fear and embracing change. By embodying

Seneca's teachings, she overcame adversity and made significant contributions to society, inspiring countless others to do the same.

Nelson Mandela: Stoicism in the Face of Adversity

Nelson Mandela, the anti-apartheid revolutionary and former President of South Africa, exhibited remarkable Stoic qualities throughout his life, particularly during his 27-year imprisonment. He once said, "I learned that courage was not the absence of fear, but the triumph over it." Mandela's ability to endure hardship and maintain his principles in the face of adversity is a testament to the power of Stoicism and Seneca's wisdom.

Why should you care about Nelson Mandela's story? His life demonstrates the resilience and inner strength that can be developed by applying Seneca's teachings. By maintaining a Stoic mindset and overcoming fear, Mandela was able to lead South Africa toward a more just and equitable future.

How have organizations and societies used Seneca's principles to create meaningful change? This question leads us to explore case studies highlighting the real-life applications of Seneca's wisdom.

Case Studies: How Organizations and Societies Have Used Seneca's Principles

Applying Stoic Principles In Education

Consider a school that sought to improve students' emotional well-being and academic performance by incorporating Stoic principles into its curriculum. By teaching students about Seneca's wisdom and the importance of overcoming fear, the school aimed to foster resilience, self-awareness, and emotional intelligence in its students.

Why should you care about this case study? It demonstrates the potential for Seneca's teachings to be applied on a broader scale, impacting not only individuals but entire communities. The school's initiative significantly improved students' well-being and academic success, highlighting the transformative power of Stoicism when integrated into educational settings.

A Company Embracing Seneca's Wisdom For Employee Well-Being

Next, let's examine a company that embraced Seneca's wisdom to promote employee well-being and cultivate a healthier work culture. By incorporating mindfulness, meditation, and Stoic teachings into their wellness program, the company aimed to help employees overcome fear, manage stress, and find a greater sense of purpose in their work.

Why should you care about this case study? It showcases the practical application of Seneca's wisdom in a corporate setting, emphasizing the potential for his teachings to benefit people from all walks of life. As a result of the program, the company saw significant improvements in employee morale, productivity, and overall well-being, demonstrating the positive impact of embracing Stoicism in the workplace.

By examining these personal anecdotes, historical figures, and case studies, it's clear that Seneca's wisdom continues to resonate in our modern world. Individuals, organizations, and societies can experience profound growth and transformation by overcoming fear and embracing reality.

As you continue to apply the lessons from Seneca's teachings to your own life, what steps can you take to ensure that your newfound wisdom is sustained and nurtured? This question leads us to consider strategies for maintaining progress and embracing a life of continuous growth and self-discovery.

CHAPTER 7.
CULTIVATING A STOIC MINDSET IN RELATIONSHIPS AND COMMUNICATION

The Importance of Empathy and Understanding in Relationships

In a world where personal connections are increasingly crucial, empathy and understanding are vital components of any healthy relationship. So, why are empathy and understanding so important in relationships?

Firstly, they foster a sense of trust and safety, allowing both individuals to feel more comfortable sharing their thoughts, feelings, and experiences. This openness enables a deeper connection between two people, leading to greater emotional intimacy.

Secondly, empathy and understanding help reduce misunderstandings and conflicts in relationships. By putting ourselves in another person's shoes and considering their feelings and perspectives, we are more likely to respond with compassion and patience.

Lastly, empathy and understanding promote personal growth. These qualities encourage us to challenge our beliefs, assumptions, and biases, allowing us to learn from others and expand our worldview.

But how can we cultivate empathy and understanding in our relationships? And how can Stoicism help us achieve this?

Strengthening Connections through Active Listening and Effective Communication

Active listening and effective communication are essential for nurturing empathy and understanding in relationships. By developing these skills, we can strengthen our connections with others and create a more harmonious environment for growth.

Active listening involves giving our full attention to the person we're communicating with without interrupting or planning our response in advance. Doing so shows that we genuinely care about their thoughts and feelings.

Here are some tips for practicing active listening:

Maintain eye contact and use open body language

Nod and make affirmative noises to show you're engaged

Summarize and paraphrase what the other person has said to ensure you understand their message

Ask open-ended questions to encourage further discussion

On the other hand, effective communication involves expressing our thoughts and feelings clearly and respectfully.

Achieving effective communication can be done by:

Using "I" statements to express your feelings without blaming or accusing the other person

Being mindful of your tone and body language

Being specific and concise in your communication

Practicing assertiveness, which means standing up for your rights and needs while respecting the rights and needs of others

How can Stoicism assist us in improving our active listening and communication skills?

Applying Stoic Principles to Conflict Resolution

Conflict is inevitable in any relationship. However, by applying Stoic principles to conflict resolution, we can navigate these challenges more effectively and maintain a strong connection with our loved ones.

A fundamental Stoic principle that we can apply to conflict resolution is focusing on what we can control. We cannot control the other person's thoughts, feelings, or actions in any disagreement. However, we can control our reactions and responses. By recognizing this, we can approach conflicts calmly and rationally, reducing the likelihood of further escalation.

Another Stoic principle that can help resolve conflicts is practicing detachment. Detachment involves recognizing that external events, such as someone else's opinions or actions, do not have the power to disturb our inner peace unless we allow them to. By maintaining a sense of detachment, we can respond to conflicts without becoming overly emotional or reactive, leading to more productive and respectful conversations.

Lastly, Stoicism encourages us to practice forgiveness and compassion toward ourselves and others. In conflicts, it's crucial to remember that everyone makes mistakes and that holding onto resentment only harms our well-being in the long run. We can let go of grudges, move forward, and foster healthier relationships by embracing forgiveness and compassion.

But how can we create an environment where healthy and supportive relationships thrive?

Fostering Healthy and Supportive Relationships

Creating a nurturing environment that promotes open communication, mutual respect, and personal growth is essential to cultivate healthy and supportive relationships.

Here are some strategies for fostering such relationships:

Establish healthy boundaries: Setting clear boundaries in relationships is crucial for maintaining balance and ensuring both parties feel respected and valued. Communicate your needs, preferences, and limits, and encourage your loved ones to do the same. Understanding and respecting each other's boundaries creates a foundation for a healthy and supportive relationship.

Encourage personal growth: Support your loved ones in their pursuit of self-improvement and personal development. Share resources, engage in stimulating conversations, and celebrate their achievements. Encourage them to pursue their passions and be open to learning from them.

Practice gratitude and appreciation: Regularly express gratitude and appreciation for the people in your life. Acknowledge their positive qualities, efforts, and contributions to your well-being. Doing so strengthens your connection and helps build a positive and supportive relationship atmosphere.

Cultivate a growth mindset: Embrace a growth mindset by believing we can develop our abilities and intelligence through hard work, dedication, and perseverance. By adopting this mindset, you and your loved ones can view challenges and setbacks as opportunities for growth and learning, fostering resilience and adaptability in your relationships.

Be a source of support and encouragement: Offer a listening ear, a shoulder to lean on, or a helping hand when your loved ones need it. Validate their feelings, offer encouragement, and provide constructive feedback when appropriate. By being a reliable source of support, you contribute to developing a strong and lasting bond.

As we apply Stoic principles and these strategies to our relationships, we can expect to see a remarkable transformation in the quality of our connections. By cultivating empathy, understanding, active listening, effective communication, and conflict resolution skills, we can build healthy and supportive relationships that enrich our lives and contribute to our overall well-being.

So, how can we ensure that we continue to apply these principles and strategies in our daily lives, and what might be the long-term benefits of doing so?

CHAPTER 8.
BALANCING WORK, PASSION, AND PERSONAL GROWTH

*The Role of Purpose and Passion
in a Fulfilling Career*

In today's fast-paced world, striking the right balance between work, passion, and personal growth can be daunting. However, it is essential to recognize the significance of these elements in living a fulfilling and meaningful life. A career driven by purpose and passion not only leads to professional success but also contributes to personal satisfaction and well-being.

The power of purpose: When you align your work with your purpose, you're more likely to feel motivated, engaged, and committed to your tasks. A clear sense of purpose provides direction and helps you make informed choices that lead to a more satisfying career path.

Unleashing your passion: Passion fuels creativity, innovation, and resilience, enabling you to overcome obstacles and persist in the face of challenges. When you are passionate about your work, you are more likely to derive a sense of joy and accomplishment from your endeavors.

To harness the potential of purpose and passion in your career, consider these strategies:

Reflect on your values, interests, and strengths: Take time to introspect and identify what truly matters to you. Assess your core values, interests, and strengths, and use these insights to guide your career choices.

Explore different opportunities: Be open to experimenting with various roles, industries, and work environments. Engaging in such exploration will allow you to understand your preferences better and help you discover your passion.

Set meaningful goals: Establish specific, measurable goals aligned with your purpose and passion. Regularly review and adjust your goals to ensure they continue to reflect your evolving aspirations and priorities.

Navigating the Challenges of Work-Life Balance

As you pursue a fulfilling career, it is essential to strike a healthy work-life balance. Achieving this balance can help prevent burnout, reduce stress, and enhance overall well-being.

Here are some tips to help you navigate the challenges of work-life balance:

Set boundaries: Clearly define the limits between your work and personal life. Establish routines and rituals that help you disconnect from work and focus on your personal life, such as turning off work notifications during evenings and weekends.

Prioritize self-care: Make time for activities that nourish your mind, body, and spirit, such as exercise, meditation, hobbies, and socializing with friends and family. Taking care of yourself enables you to be more productive, focused, and present in all aspects of your life.

Develop time management skills: Efficiently manage your time by setting priorities, breaking tasks into smaller steps, and delegating when necessary. Adopting these time management strategies will help you allocate sufficient time for your professional and personal commitments.

Prioritizing Personal Growth and Well-Being

In addition to fostering a fulfilling career and maintaining a work-life balance, it is vital to prioritize personal growth and well-being. By continually investing in yourself, you can enhance your skills, expand your knowledge, and improve your overall quality of life.

Consider the following strategies:

Pursue lifelong learning: Continuously seek opportunities to learn and grow, such as attending workshops, taking online courses, or reading books. Engaging in these activities helps you stay relevant in your field and fosters a sense of accomplishment and personal satisfaction.

Seek feedback and mentorship: Regularly solicit feedback from your colleagues, superiors, and mentors to identify areas for improvement and gain valuable insights. Embrace constructive criticism and use it as a catalyst for growth and development.

Cultivate resilience: Develop coping strategies to manage stress, setbacks, and challenges. Incorporating practices such as mindfulness, building a strong support network, and adopting a growth mindset can help you navigate these difficulties.

Embracing Change and Adapting to Life's Transitions

Change is inevitable, and adapting to life's transitions is crucial to personal growth. Embracing change can help you remain flexible, resilient, and open to new opportunities.

Here are some strategies to help you navigate change and adapt to life's transitions:

Maintain a positive attitude: Adopt an optimistic outlook and focus on the benefits and opportunities that change can bring. Cultivating a positive attitude can help you overcome challenges and emerge stronger from difficult situations.

Be proactive: Instead of passively waiting for change, take the initiative to shape your life and career. Actively seek new experiences, broaden your horizons, and embrace opportunities for growth and development.

Develop a support network: Surround yourself with supportive individuals who can provide guidance, encouragement, and a sounding board during times of change. These supportive people may include friends, family, mentors, or professional networks.

Practice adaptability: Cultivate the ability to adjust your thoughts, behaviors, and emotions in response to changing circumstances. Adapting in this way includes being open to new ideas, embracing uncertainty, and learning from your experiences.

In conclusion, balancing work, passion, and personal growth is a complex yet rewarding endeavor. By aligning your career with your purpose and passion, maintaining a healthy work-life balance, prioritizing personal growth and well-being, and embracing change and adapting to life's transitions, you can pave the way for a more fulfilling and meaningful life.

So, as you move forward, how will you apply the insights gained from this chapter to create a harmonious balance between your professional and personal life? How will you prioritize your personal growth and well-being while pursuing your passions and purpose?

The Ongoing Journey Toward A Fulfilling Life

As you continue to apply the lessons gleaned from Seneca's wisdom, it's essential to recognize that the journey toward a fulfilling life is an ongoing process. Personal growth and self-discovery require patience, commitment, and persistence.

In this pursuit, the following strategies can help you maintain progress and foster continuous growth:

Stay Curious and Open to Learning: Keep an open mind and a curious attitude. Always be willing to learn from your experiences and the wisdom of others. Embracing personal growth will allow you to grow continually and adapt to life's challenges.

Cultivate a Support Network: Surround yourself with like-minded individuals who share your values and support your journey toward personal growth. They can provide encouragement, guidance, and a sense of community as you navigate the challenges of self-discovery.

Practice Regular Self-Reflection: Engage in regular self-reflection to assess your progress and identify areas for improvement. This practice will help you stay aligned with your purpose, passions, and values, ensuring you continue living a fulfilling life.

Embrace Change and Adaptability: Be willing to embrace change and adapt to new circumstances. Recognize that personal growth often involves stepping outside your comfort zone and confronting your fears. By becoming adaptable, you'll equip yourself better to face life's uncertainties and continue toward fulfillment.

Celebrate Your Achievements: Acknowledge and celebrate your successes, big and small. Recognizing your accomplishments builds confidence and fosters a sense of self-worth, motivating you to continue your personal growth and fulfillment journey.

As you progress on your path towards a fulfilling life, remember that the wisdom of Seneca and the teachings of Stoicism can serve as a powerful guide. By understanding and applying these principles, you can cultivate resilience, self-awareness, and emotional intelligence, allowing you to overcome fear and live a life driven by purpose and passion.

While the journey may not always be smooth, embracing the wisdom of Seneca and the Stoic philosophy will empower you to face life's challenges with grace, courage, and wisdom. As you progress, you will discover that living a fulfilling life is not a destination but an ongoing process of growth, self-discovery, and personal transformation.

Finally, let us reflect on the words of Seneca himself, who wrote:

"It is not because things are difficult that we do not dare; it is because we do not dare that they are difficult."

Armed with the knowledge and insights we have gained from exploring Seneca's wisdom, we can now dare to face our fears, embrace reality, and embark on the exciting journey of finding our purpose and living fulfilling lives.

As you continue to apply the lessons of Seneca's teachings, may your journey be filled with personal growth, wisdom, and an unwavering dedication to living a life that is true to your values, passions, and purpose. Keep asking questions, stay curious, and never stop learning. Remember that the journey towards a fulfilling life is ongoing, and you are not alone.

Thank you for joining me in exploring Seneca's wisdom and its application to finding our purpose and living fulfilling lives. I hope this book has provided valuable insights and practical tools to help you face your fears, embrace reality, and continue your journey toward personal growth and self-discovery.

I wish you all the best as you continue to embrace the wisdom of Seneca and strive to live a life driven by purpose and passion.

John Sanchez
April 2023

APPENDICES

Recommended Resources For Further Reading

Throughout this book, we have explored the wisdom of Seneca and its application to overcoming fear, finding purpose, and living fulfilling lives. We recommend the following resources for those interested in delving deeper into these topics and expanding their understanding of Stoicism and personal development:

"Letters from a Stoic" by Seneca: This classic work provides insight into the thoughts and teachings of Seneca. The letters cover many topics, including overcoming fear, cultivating resilience, and embracing adversity.

"Meditations" by Marcus Aurelius: This personal journal of the Roman Emperor offers profound reflections on Stoic philosophy, personal growth, and the pursuit of wisdom. It is an invaluable resource for anyone seeking to apply Stoic principles in their daily lives.

"The Obstacle Is the Way: The Timeless Art of Turning Trials into Triumph" by Ryan Holiday: This modern interpretation of Stoic philosophy offers practical advice for overcoming obstacles, developing resilience, and turning adversity into opportunity.

"Man's Search for Meaning" by Viktor E. Frankl: This powerful book, written by a Holocaust survivor and psychiatrist, explores the importance of finding meaning and purpose in life, even in the most challenging circumstances.

"The Power of Now: A Guide to Spiritual Enlightenment" by Eckhart Tolle: This groundbreaking work teaches readers how to cultivate mindfulness and live in the present moment, fostering a greater sense of peace, contentment, and self-awareness.

"Daring Greatly: How the Courage to Be Vulnerable Transforms the Way We Live, Love, Parent, and Lead" by Brené Brown: This insightful book explores the transformative power of vulnerability and offers guidance on embracing our fears, taking risks, and living authentic lives.

As you continue your journey toward personal growth and self-discovery, these resources will serve as valuable tools for deepening your understanding of the principles and practices discussed in this book. By broadening your knowledge and expanding your perspective, you will be better equipped to face your fears, find your purpose, and live a fulfilling life.

Practical Exercises And Activities To Help Face Fears And Find Purpose

In addition to further reading, incorporating practical exercises and activities into your daily routine can help you apply the teachings of Seneca and foster personal growth.

We have designed the following exercises and activities to help you confront your fears, discover your purpose, and embrace a fulfilling life:

Fear-setting exercise: Inspired by Tim Ferriss, this exercise involves identifying your fears, assessing the potential consequences, and developing a plan to overcome them. By facing your fears head-on, you can cultivate resilience and break free from the limitations imposed by fear.

Gratitude journal: Cultivate an attitude of gratitude by maintaining a daily journal in which you record three things you are grateful for. This practice can help shift your focus from what you lack to what you have, fostering a greater sense of contentment and appreciation for life.

Values clarification: Identify your core values and use them to guide decisions and set goals. You will find meaning and purpose in your life by aligning your actions with your values.

Meditation and mindfulness practice: Develop a daily meditation practice to cultivate mindfulness and self-awareness. By learning to be present at the moment, you can better manage your fears, gain clarity on your purpose, and live a more fulfilling life.

Goal-setting and action planning: Set realistic and achievable goals that align with your values, passions, and purpose. Develop an action plan to help you stay focused and accountable as you work towards your goals.

Personal SWOT analysis: Conduct a personal SWOT (Strengths, Weaknesses, Opportunities, and Threats) analysis to gain insight into your unique abilities, areas for growth, and potential avenues for personal development. By understanding your strengths and weaknesses, you can create a plan to leverage your talents and overcome your limitations.

Visualizing success: Practice visualizing yourself successfully, facing your fears, and achieving your goals. This mental rehearsal can help build confidence, reduce anxiety, and prepare you for real-life challenges.

Embracing vulnerability: Engage in activities that require vulnerability, such as sharing your feelings with a trusted friend, participating in a public speaking event, or trying something new. Regularly facing your fears and embracing vulnerability can develop resilience and help you grow.

Seeking feedback and mentorship: Reach out to mentors,

coaches, or trusted friends for guidance and feedback on your journey toward personal growth and self-discovery. Their insights and support can be invaluable in helping you face your fears, find your purpose, and achieve your goals.

Regular self-reflection: Set aside time each week for self-reflection, during which you assess your progress, identify areas for growth, and celebrate your successes. By cultivating self-awareness, you can better understand your fears, values, and passions, enabling you to live a life that is true to your purpose.

These practical exercises and activities can help you apply the wisdom of Seneca and the principles of Stoicism in your daily life. By consistently practicing these techniques, you will equip yourself better to face your fears, discover your purpose, and embrace a fulfilling life.

Remember that personal growth and self-discovery are ongoing processes, and you must be patient with yourself as you progress. The journey may be challenging at times, but the rewards of living a life driven by purpose and passion are well worth the effort.

As you continue to apply the lessons and insights gained from this book, may you find the courage to face your fears, the wisdom to embrace reality, and the resilience to persist in your pursuit of personal growth and self-discovery. Embrace the journey, and never stop learning, growing, and striving for a life filled with purpose and fulfillment.

ACKNOWLEDGEMENT

Grateful For The Journey: Thanking Those Who Contributed To The Creation Of This Guide

Creating a book is a collaborative effort that requires the support and contributions of many individuals. I want to take a moment to express my deepest gratitude to everyone who helped make this book possible.

First and foremost, I would like to thank the team at Zunch for their hard work and dedication in bringing this book to life. From the initial brainstorming sessions to the final edits, every team member was essential in ensuring this guide was comprehensive, informative, and easy to understand.

I also want to thank my colleagues in the leadership and coaching communities for their valuable insights and feedback. Your expertise and experience were instrumental in shaping the content of this book, and I am grateful for your contributions.

Finally, I express my appreciation to the readers who provided feedback and helped us refine this guide's content. Your input has been invaluable in making this book a valuable resource for individuals seeking to find and live their purpose.

I am genuinely grateful for the support and encouragement of my family and friends throughout this process. Your unwavering support and belief in my vision have been a constant source of inspiration and motivation, and I am grateful for your encouragement every step of the way.

To the readers of this book, I express my deepest gratitude for your interest in this topic. Finding and living your purpose is one of the most important journeys you can embark upon, and I am honored to have the opportunity to share my insights and expertise with you.

In closing, I want to thank everyone who contributed to this book's creation and helped bring this vision to life. I sincerely hope this guide will serve as a valuable resource for individuals seeking to find and live their purpose and inspire you to live a fulfilling life in alignment with your unique talents, passions, and values.

Thank you for reading "Embrace the Timeless Wisdom of Seneca: Transform Your Life by Conquering Fear and Finding Purpose." We hope you found the information in this book valuable and informative.

If you have any questions or want more information about how I can help you with your journey, please don't hesitate to contact me. You can reach me through my website at www.johnsanchez.co, by phone at 972-455-4800, or by email at info@johnsanchez.co.

I am also active on social media, so please follow me on LinkedIn, Twitter, Instagram, and Facebook for the latest industry trends, job opportunities, and company news.

ABOUT THE AUTHOR

John Sanchez

Passionate About Purpose: The Background and Experience of John Sanchez, the Author

Background and Experience

As the CEO of several companies, including Zunch Digital, Zunch AI, Zunch Communications, and Zunch Staffing, I've dedicated my career to helping businesses and individuals achieve their goals. With over 25 years of experience in leadership, coaching, and human resources, I've had the privilege of working with clients from various industries, including healthcare, education, technology, and more.

As a mentor and coach, I'm passionate about helping others find and live their purpose. Everyone has a unique contribution to make to the world, and my goal is to help individuals and businesses align their actions with their purpose to create meaningful change.

Related Works and Projects

In addition to my work with Zunch-related companies, I've authored several books on leadership, coaching, and human resources. Some of my most popular works include "The Power of Purpose: A Guide to Discovering Your True Calling," "The

Leadership Playbook: Strategies for Leading in Today's Complex World," and "HR 101: A Guide to Human Resources for Small Business Owners."

I've also had the opportunity to speak at conferences and events worldwide, sharing my insights on leadership, coaching, and purpose-driven living. I'm passionate about sharing my knowledge and expertise with others, and I'm always looking for new opportunities to connect with people and help them achieve their goals.

Contact Information

If you want to learn more about my work or connect with me directly, please visit my website at johnsanchez.co. You can also connect with me on LinkedIn or Twitter for updates on my latest projects and insights.

Thank you for reading "Embrace the Timeless Wisdom of Seneca: Transform Your Life by Conquering Fear and Finding Purpose." I hope that this guide has been helpful in your journey toward finding and living your purpose, and I wish you all the best in your future endeavors.

BOOKS BY THIS AUTHOR

Unleash Your Purpose: A Step-By-Step Guide To Living A Fulfilling Life

"Unleash Your Purpose: A Step-by-Step Guide to Living a Fulfilling Life" is a comprehensive guide to discovering and living your life's purpose. In this eBook, you will learn practical strategies and tools to help you identify your unique talents, passions, and values and align them with your actions to create a meaningful and fulfilling life.

Mastering The Effective And Successful Leader Mindset

In this comprehensive guide, you'll discover the core traits of effective leaders, the art of communication, team building and management, decision-making and problem-solving skills, nurturing a results-oriented culture, leading through change and transformation, developing your personal leadership style, and balancing work and personal life.

DISCLAIMER

The information provided in this book is for informational purposes only. It should not be considered legal or professional advice. John Sanchez makes no representations or warranties of any kind, express or implied, about the completeness, accuracy, reliability, suitability, or availability with respect to the information, products, services, or related graphics contained in the book for any purpose. Therefore, any reliance on such information is strictly at your own risk.

AFTERWORD

Reflecting On Your Journey And Embracing The Future

Congratulations! As you reach the end of this book, you have taken significant steps towards understanding your fears, discovering your purpose, and embracing a fulfilling life. Your journey of self-discovery and personal growth is a continuous process, and the insights and strategies you have gained throughout these chapters are only the beginning. In this afterword, let us reflect on the lessons learned, celebrate your achievements, and consider the next steps for your ongoing journey of transformation and growth.

Revisiting Your Fears: Embracing Courage And Resilience

Throughout the book, we have discussed the nature of fear, its underlying causes, and the strategies to overcome it. By confronting your fears and understanding their roots, you have gained valuable insights into your psyche and developed the courage to face life's challenges head-on.

What changes have you noticed in your relationship with fear? As you continue on your path of self-discovery, remember to revisit your fears regularly, acknowledging your progress and celebrating your victories. Recognize the moments when you have faced your fears and emerged stronger, more resilient, and more empowered. These experiences serve as powerful reminders that you possess the inner strength to overcome obstacles and create a fulfilling, purpose-driven life.

Discovering Your Purpose: Aligning Your Life With Your Passions And Values

In the chapters devoted to purpose, we explored the importance of identifying and aligning your passions and values with your actions and decisions. By engaging in self-reflection and examining your interests, you have gained a clearer understanding of your unique purpose and the factors that drive your personal fulfillment.

How have your perspectives on purpose evolved throughout this journey? As you move forward, actively nurture your passions and remain true to your values, making choices that align with your purpose. Remember that your purpose may evolve over time, and it is essential to stay open to new experiences and opportunities that can further enhance your sense of fulfillment and meaning.

Taking Purpose-Driven Action: Empowering Yourself And Others

By embracing your purpose and using it as a driving force for change, you can create a lasting impact on your life and those around you. Throughout the book, we have discussed practical strategies for turning your dreams into reality, overcoming obstacles, and achieving your goals.

What goals have you set for yourself, and how have you made progress toward achieving them? As you continue to pursue your purpose-driven life, remember to celebrate your accomplishments and learn from your setbacks. Embrace your ability to inspire and empower others, using your purpose as a catalyst for positive change in your community and beyond.

Developing A Growth Mindset: Embracing The Journey Of Self-Discovery

One of the most valuable lessons of this book is the importance of cultivating a growth mindset. By embracing the belief that you can grow, learn, and evolve, you open yourself to a world of possibilities and opportunities for personal transformation.

How has your mindset evolved throughout this journey? As you move forward, continue to nurture your growth mindset, embracing challenges and setbacks as opportunities to learn and evolve. Recognize that your journey of self-discovery is a lifelong process, and embrace the continuous pursuit of personal growth, self-awareness, and fulfillment.

Looking Ahead: Your Ongoing Journey Of Transformation And Growth

As you close the final pages of this book, take a moment to reflect on your journey and the progress you have made. Be proud of the insights you have gained, the fears you have faced, and the steps you have taken toward discovering and embracing your purpose.

What are your next steps in your ongoing journey of transformation and growth? As you move forward, remember to revisit the lessons and strategies discussed in this book, applying them to new challenges and experiences you encounter. Keep in mind that personal growth is an ongoing process, and there will always be opportunities to learn, evolve, and adapt.

Stay curious and open to new experiences, recognizing that each adventure offers a chance to gain new insights and deepen your understanding of yourself and the world around you. Continue to seek growth opportunities through reading, attending workshops, engaging in meaningful conversations, or seeking mentorship. By embracing a lifelong commitment to personal development, you will continue to unlock your potential and create a purpose-driven life that reflects your passions and values.

Cultivating A Supportive Community: Building Connections And Sharing Your Journey

As you continue on your path of personal growth and self-discovery, remember the importance of surrounding yourself with a supportive community. Seek out like-minded individuals who share your commitment to growth and self-improvement, and cultivate relationships that foster mutual learning and encouragement.

How can you build connections and share your journey with others? Consider participating in online forums, attending local meetups, or joining clubs or organizations that align with your interests and values. By sharing your experiences, insights, and challenges with others, you gain valuable perspectives and support and have the opportunity to inspire and empower those around you.

Celebrating Your Progress And Embracing The Future

As we conclude this book, take some time to celebrate your achievements and the progress you have made. Acknowledge the hard work, courage, and determination that have brought you to this point in your journey, and honor the person you have become through your commitment to growth and self-discovery.

With a renewed sense of purpose, a deeper understanding of your fears, and a growth mindset that embraces life's challenges and opportunities, you are now equipped to forge a fulfilling, purpose-driven life that reflects your most authentic self. May your journey continue to be filled with growth, inspiration, and transformation as you embrace your purpose and share your unique gifts with the world.

So, are you ready to embark on the next chapter of your personal journey? With newfound wisdom and determination, take that first step towards a brighter, more fulfilling future, and remember that the power to create lasting change lies within you.

www.ingramcontent.com/pod-product-compliance
Lightning Source LLC
Chambersburg PA
CBHW071029220526
45467CB00004B/1587